The **Pebble** First Guide to

Whales

by Erika L. Shores

Consulting Editor: Gail Saunders-Smith, PhD

Consultant: Deborah Nuzzolo
Education Manager
SeaWorld, San Diego

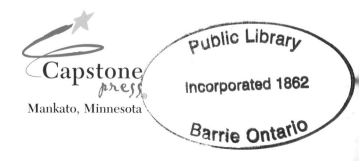

Capstone
press

Mankato, Minnesota

Pebble Books are published by Capstone Press,
151 Good Counsel Drive, P.O. Box 669, Mankato, Minnesota 56002.
www.capstonepress.com

1 2 3 4 5 6 13 12 11 10 09 08

Library of Congress Cataloging-in-Publication Data
Shores, Erika L., 1976–
    The Pebble first guide to whales / by Erika L. Shores.
        p. cm. — (Pebble books. Pebble first guides)
    Includes bibliographical references and index.
    ISBN-13: 978-1-4296-1713-0 (hardcover)
    ISBN-10: 1-4296-1713-6 (hardcover)
    ISBN-13: 978-1-4296-2807-5 (softcover pbk.)
    ISBN-10: 1-4296-2807-3 (softcover pbk.)
    1. Whales — Juvenile literature. I. Title. II. Series.
QL737.C4S4888 2009
599.5 — dc22   2008001397

Summary: A basic field guide format introduces 13 whale species. Includes color
    photographs and range maps.

About Whales

Whales are divided into two groups — toothed whales and baleen whales. Baleen whales have fringed plates in their mouths instead of teeth. The plates are called baleen.

Note to Parents and Teachers

The Pebble First Guides set supports science standards related to life science. In a reference format, this book describes and illustrates 13 whale species. This book introduces early readers to subject-specific vocabulary words, which are defined in the Glossary section. Early readers may need assistance to read some words and to use the Table of Contents, Glossary, Read More, Internet Sites, and Index sections of the book.

Table of Contents

Toothed Whales

Beluga Whale 4
Killer Whale 6
Narwhal Whale 8
Pilot Whale 10
Sperm Whale 12

Baleen Whales

Blue Whale 14
Bowhead Whale 16
Fin Whale 18
Gray Whale 20
Humpback Whale 22
Minke Whale 24
Right Whale 26
Sei Whale 28

Glossary 30
Read More 31
Internet Sites 31
Index 32

Length:	13 to 16 feet (4 to 5 meters)
Weight:	1 to 2 tons (.9 to 1.8 metric tons)
Eats:	fish, squid, shrimp, crabs
Lives:	shallow coastal waters
Facts:	• makes 11 different sounds
	• calf is gray at birth

Beluga Whale Range

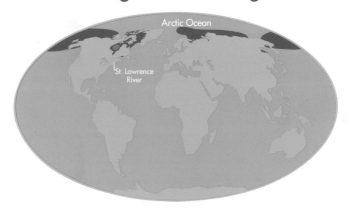

Arctic Ocean

St. Lawrence River

■ Arctic Ocean and subarctic waters,
St. Lawrence River

calf

female

Killer Whale

female and calf

Length: 16 to 28 feet (5 to 9 meters)

Weight: 4 to 6 tons (4 to 5 metric tons)

Eats: sea lions, seals, porpoises, fish

Lives: cold water

Facts:
- also called orca
- lives in pods of 5 to 30 whales

Killer Whale Range

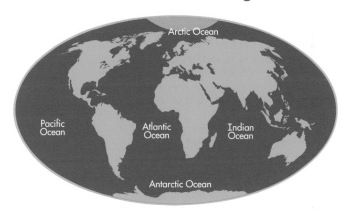

Arctic Ocean

Pacific
Ocean

Atlantic
Ocean

Indian
Ocean

Antarctic Ocean

■ all oceans

pod

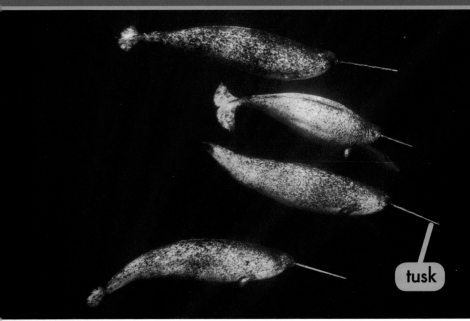

tusk

Length: 13 to 15 feet (4 to 5 meters)

Weight: 1 to 2 tons (.9 to 1.8 metric tons)

Eats: Arctic cod, squid, shrimp

Lives: deep water

Facts:
- has a long tusk
- one of the deepest-diving whales

Narwhal Whale Range

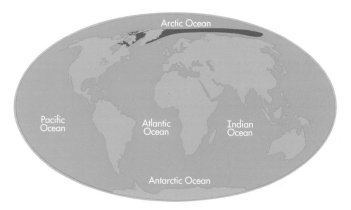

Arctic Ocean

Pacific Ocean

Atlantic Ocean

Indian Ocean

Antarctic Ocean

■ Arctic Ocean

female and calf

short-finned
pilot whale

Length:	16 to 20 feet (5 to 6 meters)
Weight:	1.5 to 3 tons (1 to 3 metric tons)
Eats:	squid, fish
Lives:	short-finned in warm water long-finned in colder water
Facts:	• lives in pods of 20 to 90 whales • hunts in pods

Pilot Whale Range

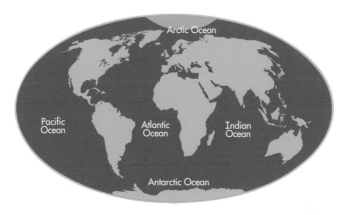

Arctic Ocean

Pacific
Ocean

Atlantic
Ocean

Indian
Ocean

Antarctic Ocean

■ all oceans

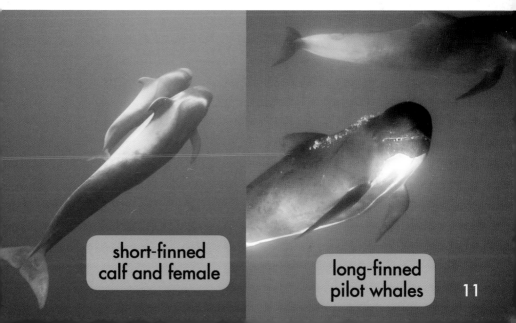

short-finned
calf and female

long-finned
pilot whales

Sperm Whale

Length: 36 to 60 feet (11 to 18 meters)

Weight: 13 to 45 tons (12 to 41 metric tons)

Eats: squid, fish, rays, sharks

Lives: deep water

Facts:
- largest whale with teeth
- can dive underwater for an hour
- endangered

Sperm Whale Range

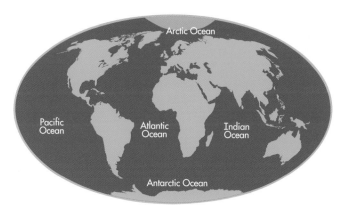

Arctic Ocean

Pacific
Ocean

Atlantic
Ocean

Indian
Ocean

Antarctic Ocean

■ all oceans

calf and female

Blue Whale

Length:	75 to 100 feet (23 to 30 meters)
Weight:	100 tons (91 metric tons)
Eats:	krill
Lives:	cold water to eat; warm water to mate
Facts:	• largest animal on earth
	• eats up to 40 million krill a day
	• endangered

Blue Whale Range

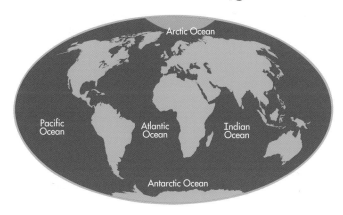

Arctic Ocean

Pacific
Ocean

Atlantic
Ocean

Indian
Ocean

Antarctic Ocean

■ all oceans

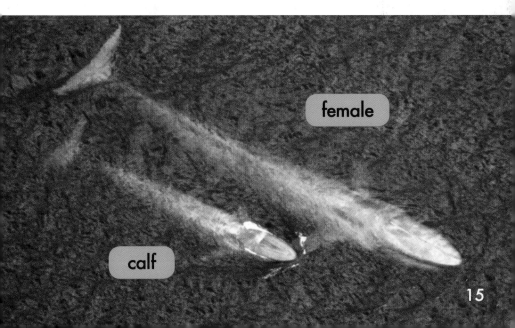

female

calf

Bowhead Whale

Length:	50 to 60 feet (15 to 18 meters)
Weight:	75 tons (68 metric tons)
Eats:	tiny crustaceans, krill
Lives:	along Arctic ice
Facts:	• large head breaks through ice
	• longest baleen plates of any whale
	• endangered

Bowhead Whale Range

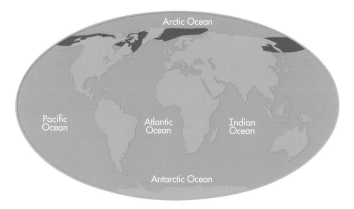

Arctic Ocean

Pacific Ocean

Atlantic Ocean

Indian Ocean

Antarctic Ocean

Arctic Ocean and subarctic waters

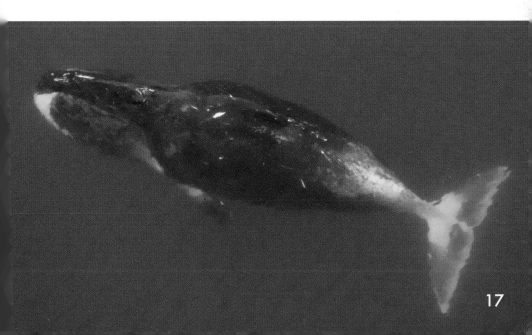

Length:	78 to 88 feet (24 to 27 meters)
Weight:	50 to 70 tons (45 to 64 metric tons)
Eats:	krill
Lives:	cold water in summer; warm water in winter
Facts:	• V-shaped head is flat on top
	• second largest animal on earth
	• endangered

Fin Whale Range

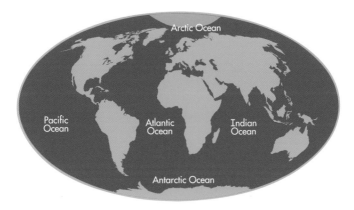

Arctic Ocean

Pacific Ocean

Atlantic Ocean

Indian Ocean

Antarctic Ocean

■ all oceans

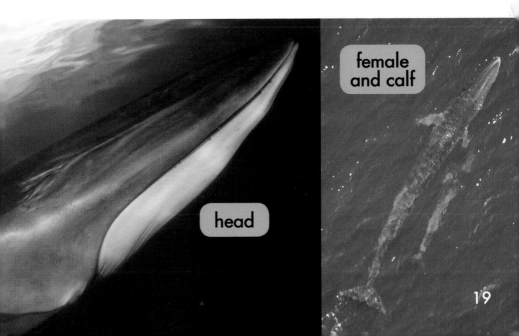

head

female and calf

Gray Whale

blowhole

Length:	45 to 50 feet (14 to 15 meters)
Weight:	30 to 40 tons (27 to 36 metric tons)
Eats:	small crustaceans
Lives:	shallow coastal waters
Facts:	• swims south to give birth
	• travels alone

Gray Whale Range

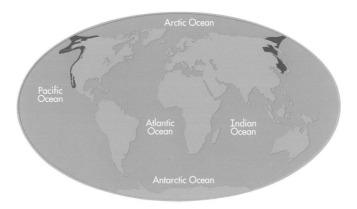

Arctic Ocean

Pacific Ocean

Atlantic Ocean

Indian Ocean

Antarctic Ocean

■ North Pacific Ocean

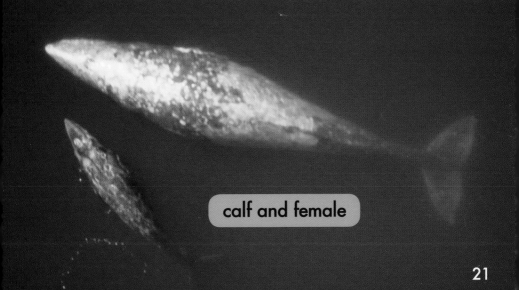

calf and female

Humpback Whale

flipper

flipper

Length:	40 to 50 feet (12 to 15 meters)
Weight:	25 to 40 tons (23 to 36 metric tons)
Eats:	krill, small fish
Lives:	cold water in summer; warm water in winter
Facts:	• male sings songs
	• longest flippers of any whale
	• endangered

Humpback Whale Range

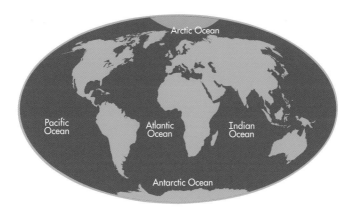

Arctic Ocean

Pacific Ocean

Atlantic Ocean

Indian Ocean

Antarctic Ocean

■ all oceans

calf and female

Length: 26 to 33 feet (8 to 10 meters)

Weight: 10 tons (9 metric tons)

Eats: krill, small fish

Lives: warm water in winter; cold in summer

Facts: • bright white patch on flippers
          • travels alone or in small groups

Minke Whale Range

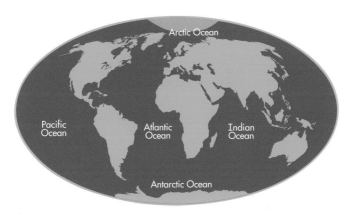

Arctic Ocean

Pacific
Ocean

Atlantic
Ocean

Indian
Ocean

Antarctic Ocean

■ all oceans

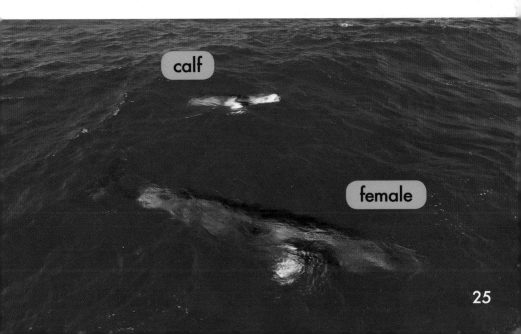

calf

female

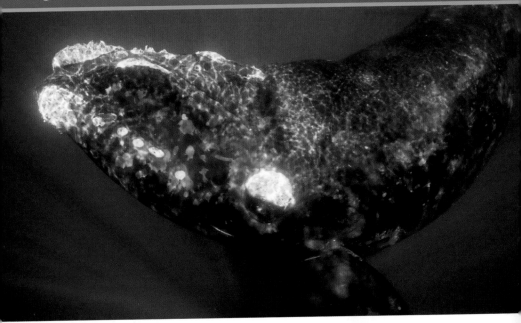

Length:	35 to 55 feet (11 to 17 meters)
Weight:	60 to 80 tons (54 to 73 metric tons)
Eats:	krill, small crustaceans
Lives:	cold water to eat; warm water to mate
Facts:	• wartlike bumps grow on head • white patch on belly • endangered

Right Whale Range

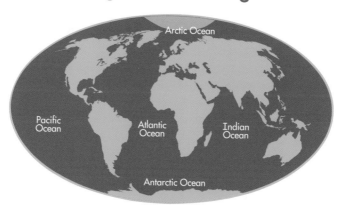

Arctic Ocean

Pacific
Ocean

Atlantic
Ocean

Indian
Ocean

Antarctic Ocean

■ all oceans

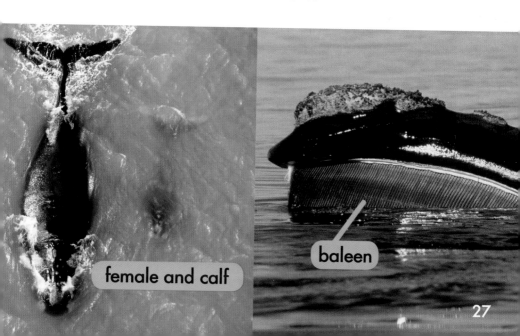

female and calf

baleen

Length: 45 to 65 feet (14 to 20 meters)

Weight: 20 to 50 tons (18 to 45 metric tons)

Eats: small crustaceans, plankton

Lives: deep water

Facts: • one of the fastest baleen whales

            • lives alone or in small groups

            • endangered

Sei Whale Range

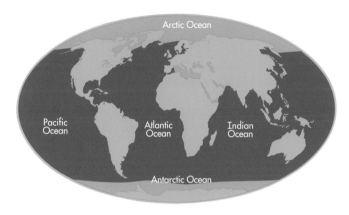

Arctic Ocean

Pacific Ocean

Atlantic Ocean

Indian Ocean

Antarctic Ocean

■ Pacific, Atlantic, and Indian oceans

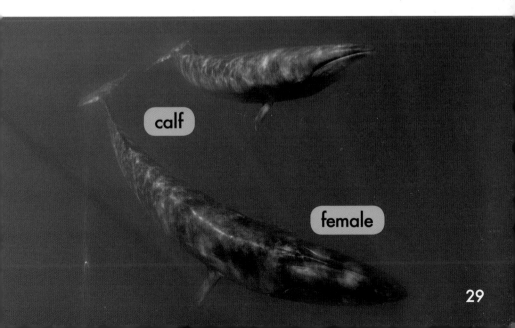

calf

female

Glossary

baleen — rows of fringed plates in the mouth; baleen whales filter water through their mouth to catch fish, krill, or plankton in their baleen.

blowhole — a hole on top of a whale's head; whales breathe air through blowholes.

crustacean — a sea animal with an outer skeleton; a crab is a crustacean.

endangered — at risk of dying out

flipper — a paddlelike body part on a whale's side; flippers help whales steer through water.

krill — tiny shrimplike animals

plankton — very tiny plants and animals that drift in the water

pod — a large group of whales; whales in a pod are usually related to each other.

subarctic — areas directly south of the Arctic Circle; the Arctic Circle is an imaginary line just south of the North Pole.

tusk — a long, pointed tooth

Read More

Lindeen, Carol K. *Whales*. Under the Sea. Mankato, Minn.: Capstone Press, 2005.

Simon, Seymour. *Whales*. New York: Collins, 2006.

Smith, Molly. *Blue Whale: The World's Biggest Mammal*. SuperSized! New York: Bearport, 2007.

Internet Sites

FactHound offers a safe, fun way to find Internet sites related to this book. All of the sites on FactHound have been researched by our staff.

Here's how:

1. Visit *www.facthound.com*
2. Choose your grade level.
3. Type in this book ID **1429617136** for age-appropriate sites. You may also browse subjects by clicking on letters, or by clicking on pictures and words.
4. Click on the **Fetch It** button.

FactHound will fetch the best sites for you!

Index

baleen, 16, 27, 28
blowholes, 20
crustaceans, 4, 16, 20, 26, 28
diving, 8, 12
endangered, 12, 14, 16 18, 22, 26, 28
flippers, 22, 24

heads, 18, 26
krill, 14, 16, 18, 22, 24, 26
mating, 14, 26
pods, 6, 10
songs, 22
teeth, 12
tusks, 8

Grade: 1
Early-Intervention Level: 24

Editorial Credits
Alison Thiele and Juliette Peters, designers; Danielle Ceminsky, map illustrator; Jo Miller, photo researcher

Photo Credits
BigStockPhoto.com/Nicholas Pix, cover (beluga whale)
Bruce Coleman Inc./Tom Brakefield, 22
Getty Images Inc./Discovery Channel Images/Jeff Foott, 20; Minden Pictures/ Flip Nicklin, 5, 8, 15; Photographer's Choice/Thomas Schmitt, 11 (left); Science Faction Flip Nicklin, 26
iStockphoto/Matthew Hull, cover (humpback whale)
Jupiter Images/Workbook Stock, 23
Minden Pictures/Flip Nicklin, 17; Frans Lanting, 21
Nature Picture Library/Doc White, 13; Doug Allan, 9; Doug Perrine, 28, 29; Jurgen Freund, 25; Mark Carwardine, 19 (right); Martha Holmes, 16
Peter Arnold/Biosphoto/Gohier Francois, 7, 14; Gerald Soury, 10; Harpe, 27 (left); Jonathan Bird, 12; Kelvin Aitken, 24
Seapics/Jens Kuhfs, 11 (right), 18; Mark Jones, 19 (left)
Shutterstock/Anson Hung, cover (killer whale); Jan Daly, 6
SuperStock Inc./Pacific Stock, cover (sperm whale)
Visuals Unlimited/David Fleetham, 4; James Watt, 27 (right)